THE HOSPITAL BEDSIDE BOOK

The
HOSPITAL BEDSIDE BOOK

Duncan B Heriot

THE SAINT ANDREW PRESS
EDINBURGH

© Duncan B Heriot

First published in 1966 by
THE DRUMMOND TRUST
Republished in 1984, 1990 by
THE SAINT ANDREW PRESS
121 George Street
Edinburgh EH2 4YN

ISBN 0 7152 0576 5

The Publisher acknowledges financial assistance from
The Drummond Trust
towards the publication of this volume.

This book has been set in 11/12 pt Palatino.
Cover design by Mark Blackadder.
Printed and Bound in Great Britain by
Athenaeum Press Ltd., Newcastle upon Tyne.

FOREWORD
(to the original edition)

A spell in hospital has led me to compile this book in the hope that it would meet, what I feel to be, a definite need. For, despite the number of beds in the ward, the devoted service of the nurses, and the trained skill of the doctors, every patient has an inner sense of isolation and loneliness of spirit. Visiting hours are eagerly awaited, when loved ones come bringing flowers and gifts, but even more important, bringing news of home, and linking us up with the life from which we feel cut off! After they depart, we lie back and ponder with gratitude on their love, but with the removal of their presence we are conscious of a sense of depression.

Reading is a solace, but often the book is heavy and awkward to hold. Moreover, we seem to have lost our power of concentration. We can only think in 'snippets'. Even if we brought our Bibles, may of us are too unfamiliar with its 'set up' to find the passages that would bring us comfort and uplift of spirit.

It is to meet this physical, mental and spiritual need that this *Hospital Bedside Book* has been compiled. It is easy to handle. The chosen passages are deliberately brief, but they are profound in meaning. It is suggested that the patient should read a section slowly and thoughtfully. Memorise a sentence or two, then lie back and meditate on them. In a surprisingly short time, he (or she) will find he has stored his mind with helpful thoughts and provided himself with an inner strength of spirit.

Like many, when they find life overwhelming, I turned to my Bible in the trenches during the First World War, marking the verses and passages that helped me. I also began to copy out scraps of poems and prayers from various sources. Many of these are included in this book, and I trust others will also find them a source of strength. Unfortunately, I did not always keep a note of the author. Thus, I have been unable to trace the sources of the verses, 'As for God, his way is Perfect,' and if I have infringed copyright, I would ask to be forgiven.

The prayers have been chosen from those composed by 'Saints of God' down the centuries. To avoid infringing on copyright none has been taken from the many inspiring 'Books of Prayers' by modern writers, but if anywhere in this book I have so infringed, I would crave forgiveness in view of the purpose for which it has been compiled.

D B Heriot

THE HOSPITAL BEDSIDE BOOK

'Lord, teach us to pray.'

The Lord's Prayer

Our Father, which art in Heaven,
Hallowed be thy Name.
Thy Kingdom come.
Thy will be done
In Earth, as it is in Heaven.
Give us this day our daily bread.
And forgive us our trespasses,
As we forgive them that trespass against us,
And lead us not into temptation;
But deliver us from evil;
For thine is the Kingdom,
The Power and the Glory,
For ever and ever. Amen.

FIRST DAY

Fear not: when thou passest through the waters, I will be with thee: and through the rivers, they shall not overflow thee.

> Art thou afraid his power shall fail
> When comes thy evil day?
> And can an all-creating arm
> Grow weary or decay?

Say to yourself:

> (1) I am here by God's appointment.
> (2) I am here in God's keeping.
> (3) I am here under his training.
> (4) I am here for his time.

Daily Reading
Romans 8 (selected)

And we know that all things work together for good to them that love God, to them who are called according to his purpose.

What shall we say then to these things? If God be for us, who can be against us?

Who shall seperate us from the love of Christ? Shall tribulation, or distress, or persecution, or famine, or nakedness, or peril, or sword?

Nay, in all these things we are more than conquerors through him that loved us.

For I am persuaded, that neither death, nor life, nor angels, nor principalities, nor powers, nor things present, nor things to come, nor height, nor depth, nor any other creature, shall be able to seperate us from the love of God, which is in Christ Jesus our Lord.

Prayers
In the morning

O God our Father, what is before us, we know not, but this we do know, that all things are ordered with unerring wisdom and unbounded love, by thee our God, who art love. Grant us in all things to see thy hand; through Jesus Christ our Lord. Amen.

Revd Charles Simeon, 1759-1836

In the evening

O Lord God Almighty, who givest power to the faint, and increasest strength to them that no might; without thee we can do nothing, but by thy gracious assistance we are enabled for whatever may be laid upon us. Lord of Power and Love, we come, trusting in thine Almighty strength, and thine Infinite goodness, to ask from thee what is wanting in ourselves; even that grace which shall help us to be, as thou would'st have us be. Our God, let thy grace be sufficient for us, and ever present with us, that we do all the things as we ought. We trust in thee, in whom is everlasting strength. Be thou our helper, to carry us beyond our own strength, and make all that we think, and speak, and do, acceptable in thy sight, through Jesus Christ. Amen.

Revd Benjamin Jenks, 1646-1724

SECOND DAY

Behold a man shall be as an hiding place from the wind, and a covert from the tempest, as rivers of water in a dry place, as the shadow of a great rock in a weary land.

Yea, through life, death, through sorrow and through sinning,
He shall suffice me for he hath sufficed:
Christ is the end, for Christ was the beginning,
Christ the beginning, for the end is Christ.

Daily Reading
Psalm 121

I will lift up mine eyes unto the hills, from whence cometh my help.

My help cometh from the Lord, which made heaven and earth.

He will not suffer thy foot to be moved: he that keepeth Israel shall neither slumber nor sleep.

The Lord is thy keeper, the Lord is thy shade upon thy right hand.

The sun shall not smite thee by day nor the moon by night.

The Lord shall preserve thee from all evil: he shall preserve thy soul.

The Lord shall preserve thy going out and thy coming in from this time forth, and even for evermore.

Prayers
In the morning

O thou divine Spirit that, in all events of life art knocking at the door of my heart, help me to respond to thee. I would take the events of my life as good and perfect gifts from thee: I would perceive even the sorrows of life as distinguished gifts from thee. I would have my heart ever open to thee. Whether thou comest to me in sunshine, or in pain, I would take thee into my heart joyfully. Thou art thyself more than the sunshine, thou art thyself compensation for the rain; it is thee and not thy gifts I crave; through Jesus Christ our Lord. Amen.

George Matheson, 1842-1906

In the evening

O Lord, who art the shadow of a great rock in a weary land, who beholdest thy weak creatures weary of labour, weary of pleasures, weary of heart, and weary of self. In thine abundant compassion and unutterable tenderness bring us, we pray thee unto thy rest; through Jesus Christ, thy Son, our Saviour. Amen.

Christina G Rossetti, 1830-1894

THIRD DAY

I will be with thee: I will not fail thee, nor forsake thee.

The day is long and the day is hard;
We are tired of the march and of keeping
    guard,
Tired of the sense of a fight to be won,
Of days to live through and of work to be
    done:
Yet all the while did we only see
We walk in the Lord's own company.

Daily Reading
Joshua 1 (selected)

The Lord spake unto Joshua saying, As I was with Moses, so I will be with thee. Be strong and of a good courage, that thou mayest observe to do according to all the law, which Moses my servant commanded thee: turn not from it to the right hand or to the left, that thou mayest prosper whithersoever thou goest.

    This book of the law shall not depart out of thy mouth; but thou shalt meditate therein day and night, that thou mayest observe to do according to all that is written therein: for then thou shalt make thy way prosperous and then thou shalt have good success.

Have I not commanded thee? Be strong and of a good courage; be not afraid, neither be thou dismayed: for the Lord thy God is with thee whithersoever thou goest.

Prayers
In the morning

Into thy hands, O God, we commend ourselves and all who are dear to us this day. Let the gift of thy special Presence be with us even unto its close. Grant us never to lose sight of thee all the day long, so that at eventide we may again give thanks unto thee; through Jesus Christ our Lord. Amen.

Gelasian Sacramentary, 494

In the evening

Christ be with me, Christ within me,
Christ before me, Christ beside me,
Christ to win me.
Christ to comfort and restore me,
Christ beneath me, Christ above me,
Christ in quiet, Christ in danger,
Christ in hearts of all that love me,
Christ in mouth of friend and strangers.

The 'Breastplate' of St Patrick, c. 389-461

FOURTH DAY

The angel of the Lord encampeth round about them that fear him, and delivereth them.

> I may not bid the shadows flee—
> They are the shadows of thy wing:
> Give but the eye more power to see
> The love behind their gathering.

Daily Reading
Psalm 34 (selected)

O magnify the Lord with me, and let us exalt his name together.

I sought the Lord, and he heard me, and delivered me from all my fears.

They looked unto him, and were lightened: and their faces were not ashamed.

This poor man cried, and the Lord heard him, and saved him out of all his troubles.

O taste and see that the Lord is good: blessed is the man that trusteth in him.

The eyes of the Lord are upon the righteous, and his ears are open unto their cry.

The righteous cry, and the Lord heareth, and delivereth them out of their troubles.

The Lord is nigh unto them that are of a broken heart: and saveth such as be of a contrite spirit.

The Lord redeemeth the soul of his servants: and none of them that trust in him shall be desolate.

Prayers
In the morning

We beseech thee , O Lord and Master, to be our help and succour. Save those who are in tribulation; have mercy on the lonely; lift up the fallen; show thyself unto the needy; heal the suffering; convert the wanderers; feed the hungry; raise up the weak; comfort the faint-hearted.

Let all people know that thou art God alone, that Jesus Christ is thy Son, and that we are thy people and the sheep of thy pasture; for the sake of Jesus Christ. Amen.

Clement of Rome, 95

In the evening

Watch thou, dear Lord, with those who wake or watch or weep this night, and give thine angels charge over those who sleep. Tend thy sick ones, O Lord Christ. Rest thy weary ones. Bless thy dying ones. Sooth thy suffering ones. Pity thine afflicted ones. Shield thy joyous ones. And all for thy love's sake. Amen.

St Augustine, 354-430

FIFTH DAY

Trust in the Lord with all thine heart. In all thy ways acknowledge him, and he shall direct thy paths.

Our plans may be disjointed,
But we may calmly rest,
For what he hath appointed
Is better than our best.

Daily Reading
Psalm 43 and 56 (selected)

What time I am afraid, I will trust in thee.

In God have I put my trust: I will trust and
not be afraid.

Why art thou cast down, O my soul? And
why art thou disquieted within me? Hope in
God: for I shall yet praise him, who is the health
of my countenance and my God.

Habakkuk 3:17-18

For though the fig-tree shall not flourish,
Neither shall fruit be in the vines;
The labour of the olive shall fail,
And the fields shall yield no food;
The flock shall be cut off from the fold,
And there shall be no herd in the stalls:
Yet I will rejoice in the Lord,
I will joy in the God of my salvation.

Prayers
In the morning

O merciful God, be thou now unto me a strong
tower of defence, I humbly entreat thee. Give
me grace to await thy pleasure, and patiently to

bear what thou doest unto me; nothing doubting or mistrusting thy goodness towards me; for thou knowest what is good for me better than I do. Therefore do with me in all things what thou wilt; only arm me, I beseech thee, with thine armour, that I may stand fast; above all things, taking to me the shield of faith; praying always that I may refer myself wholly to thy will, abiding thy pleasure and comforting myself in those troubles which it shall please thee to send me, seeing such troubles are profitable for me; and I am assuredly persuaded that all thou doest cannot but be well; and unto thee be all honour and glory. Amen.

Lady Jane Grey, 1537-1554

In the evening

Bestow, O God, this grace upon us, that in the school of suffering we should learn self-conquest, and through sorrow learn self control.

Aeschylus, 525-426 BC

Almighty God, grant unto us who know that we are weak, and who trust in thee because we know that thou art strong, the gladsome help of thy loving kindness. Amen.

Roman Breviary

SIXTH DAY

Jesus said, 'I am the Good Shepherd: the Good Shepherd giveth his life for the sheep'.

> The King of Love my Shepherd is,
> Whose goodness faileth never;
> I nothing lack if I am his
> And he is mine for ever.
>
> Perverse and foolish oft I strayed;
> But yet in love he sought me,
> And on his shoulder gently laid,
> And home, rejoicing brought me.

Daily Reading
Psalm 23

The Lord is my Shepherd; I shall not want.
He maketh me to lie down in green pastures:
He leadeth me beside the still waters.
He restoreth my soul: he leadeth me
In the paths of righteousness for his name's sake.
Yea, though I walk through the valley of the shadow of death,
I will fear no evil: for thou art with me:
Thy rod and thy staff they comfort me.
Thou preparest a table before me in the presence of mine enemies:
Thou anointest my head with oil, my cup runneth over.
Surely goodness and mercy shall follow me
All the days of my life:
And I will dwell in the House of the Lord for ever.

Prayers
In the morning

O Lord God, in whom we live, and move, and have our being, open our eyes that we may behold thy Fatherly presence ever about us. Draw our hearts to thee with the power of thy love. Teach us to be anxious for nothing, and when we have done what thou hast given us to do, help us, O God our Saviour, to leave the issue to thy wisdom. Take from us all doubt and mistrust. Lift our thoughts up to thee and make us to know that all things are possible to us through thy son our Redeemer. Amen.

Bishop Westcott, 1825-1901

In the evening

O Lord Jesus Christ, thou Good Shepherd of the sheep, who comest to seek the lost, and gather them to thy fold, have compassion upon those who have wandered from thee; feed those who hunger, cause the weary to lie down in thy pastures, bind up those who are broken in heart, and strengthen those who are weak, that we relying on thy care and being comforted by thy love, may abide in thy guidance to our lives' end; for thy Name's sake. Amen.

Ancient Collect

SEVENTH DAY

'Comfort ye, comfort ye my people,' saith your God.

Drop thy still dews of quietness
Till all our strivings cease;
Take from our souls the strain and stress,
And let our ordered lives confess
The beauty of thy peace.

Daily Reading
Isaiah 40 (selected)

Behold, the Lord God will come with strong hand, and his arm shall rule for him: behold, his reward is with him, and his work before him.

He shall feed his flock like a shepherd: he shall gather the lambs with his arm, and carry them in his bosom, and shall gently lead them that are with young.

To whom then will you liken me, or shall I be equal? saith the Holy One.

Hast thou not known? Hast thou not heard, that the everlasting God, the Lord, the Creator of the ends of the earth, fainteth not, neither is weary? There is no searching of his understanding.

He giveth power to the faint; and to them that have no might he increaseth strength.

Even the youths shall faint and be weary, and the young men shall utterly fall: but they that wait upon the Lord shall renew their strength; they shall mount up with wings as eagles; they shall run and not be weary; and they shall walk and not faint.

Prayers
In the morning

Relieve and comfort, O Lord, all the persecuted and afflicted: speak peace to troubled consciences: strengthen the weak: confirm the strong: instruct the ignorant: deliver the oppressed: relieve the needy: and bring us all by the waters of comfort and in the ways of righteousness to the kingdom of rest and glory; through Jesus Christ our Lord. Amen.

Jeremy Taylor, 1613-1667

In the evening

Father in heaven, to thee are known
Our many hopes and fears,
Our heavy weight of mortal toil,
  Our bitterness of tears.

For weary eyes, and aching hearts,
And feet that from thee rove,
The sick, the poor, the tired, the fallen,
  We pray thee, God of Love.

We bring to thee our hopes and fears,
And at thy footstool lay;
And Father, thou who lovest all
  Wilt hear us when we pray.

Hymn of the Calabrian Shepherds

EIGHTH DAY

Draw nigh unto God, and he will draw nigh unto you.

Spirit divine, attend our prayers,
And make our hearts thy home
Descend with all thy gracious powers,
O come, great Spirit, come.

Daily Reading
Psalm 51 (selected)

Have mercy upon me, O God, according to thy loving-kindness; according unto the multitude of thy tender mercies blot out my transgressions.

Wash me thoroughly from mine iniquity, and cleanse me from my sin.

For I acknowledge my transgressions: and my sin is ever before me.

Purge me with hyssop, and I shall be clean: wash me and I shall be whiter than snow.

Hide thy face from my sins, and blot out all mine iniquities.

Create in me a clean heart, O God; and renew a right spirit within me.

Cast me not away from thy presence; and take not thy holy spirit from me.

Restore unto me the joy of thy salvation; and uphold me with thy free spirit.

Deliver me, O God, thou God of my salvation; and my tongue shall sing aloud of thy righteousness.

O Lord, open thou my lips; and my mouth shall show forth thy praise.

Prayers
In the morning

Make us remember, O God, that every day is thy gift and ought to be used according to thy command, through Jesus Christ our Lord. Amen.

Dr Johnston, 1709-1784

Bless all who worship thee from the rising of the sun unto the going down of the same. Of thy goodness give us; with thy love inspire us; by thy power protect us; now and always. Amen.

An Ancient Collect

In the evening

Save us, O Lord, while waking and guard us while sleeping, that when we wake we may watch with Christ, and when we sleep we may rest in peace. Amen.

Roman Breviary

Lighten our darkness, we beseech thee , O Lord: and by thy great mercy defend us from all perils and dangers of this night: for the love of thy only Son, our Saviour, Jesus Christ. Amen.

Gelasian Sacramentary, 494

NINTH DAY

God shall supply all your need according to his riches in glory by Christ Jesus.

> O heavenly Love, how precious still,
> In days of weariness and ill,
> In nights of pain and helplessness,
> To heal, to comfort and to bless.
>
> O Love of God, our shield and stay
> Through all the perils of the way;
> Eternal Love, in thee we rest,
> For ever safe, for ever blest.

Daily Reading
Philippians 4 (selected)

Rejoice in the Lord always: and again I say, rejoice. Be careful for nothing; but in everything by prayer and supplication with thanksgiving let your requests be made known unto God.

And the peace of God which passeth all understanding shall keep your hearts and minds through Christ Jesus.

Finally, whatsoever things are true, whatsoever things are honest, whatsoever things are just, whatsoever things are pure, whatsoever things are lovely, whatsoever things are of good report; if there be any virtue, and if there be any praise think on these things.

Those things, which ye have both learned, and received, and heard, and seen in me, do: and the God of peace shall be with you.

17

Prayers
In the morning

Lord make us instruments of thy peace.

> Where there is hatred, let us sow love;
> Where there is injury, pardon;
> Where there is discord, union;
> Where there is doubt, faith;
> Where there is despair, hope;
> Where there is darkness, light;
> Where there is sadness, joy:

For thy mercy and thy truth's sake. Amen.

St Francis, 1182-1226

In the evening

> May God the father bless us;
> May Christ take care of us;
> May the Holy Spirit enlighten us
> All the days of our life.

The Lord be our Defender and Keeper of body and soul now and for ever. Amen.

Aedelwald, Saxon Bishop, ninth century

TENTH DAY

*My grace is sufficient for thee: for my strength is
made perfect in weakness.*
*Strength is born in the deep silence of suffering: not
amidst joy.*

I walk a mile with Pleasure, she chatted all the
    way,
But left me none the wiser for all she had to say.
I walked a mile with Sorrow, and ne'er a work
    spake she,
But O the things I learned, when Sorrow walked
    with me.

Daily Reading
Psalm 107 (selected)

O give thanks unto the Lord, for he is good: for
his mercy endureth for ever.

For he satisfieth the longing soul, and filleth
the hungry soul with goodness.

Such as sit in darkness and in the shadow of
death, being bound in affliction and iron; they
fell down and there was none to help.

Then they cried unto the Lord in their trouble,
and he saved them out of their distresses.

He brought them out of darkness and the
shadow of death, and brake their bands in sunder.

He sent his word, and healed them, and delivered them from their destructions.

O that men would praise the Lord for his goodness, and for his wonderful works to the children of men.

Prayers
In the morning

Let thy tender mercy, O Lord. enfold the sick and suffering. Let those who are afflicted know that in quietness and confidence lieth their strength. Give them a calm trust that thou doest all things well. In thy good time and way grant them to regain health and gladness, through the love and power of our Saviour, Jesus Christ. Amen.

Revd Rowland Williams, 1818-1870

In the evening

Go with each of us to rest; if any awake temper to them the dark hours of watching; and when the day returns, return to us, our Sun and Comforter, and call us up with morning faces and with morning hearts, eager to labour, eager to be happy, if happiness should be our portion, and if the day be marked for sorrow, strong to endure it. Amen.

Robert Louis Stevenson, 1850-1894

ELEVENTH DAY

Casting all your care upon him: for he careth for you.

Absolutely tender, absolutely true,
Understanding all things, understanding
    you,
Infinitely loving, exquisitely near,
This is God our Father
What have we to fear?

Daily Reading
Matthew 6 (selected)

Therefore I say unto you, Take no thought for
your life, what ye shall eat, or what ye shall
drink; nor yet for your body, what ye shall put
on. Is not the life more than meat, and the body
than raiment?

Behold the fowls of the air: for they sow not,
neither do they reap, nor gather into barns; yet
your heavenly Father feedeth them. Are ye not
much better than they?

And why take ye thought for raiment? Con-
sider the lilies of the field, how they grow; they
toil not, neither do they spin: yet I say unto you,
that even Solomon in all his glory was not
arrayed like one of these.

Wherefore, if God so clothe the grass of the
field, which today is, and tomorrow is cast into
the oven, shall he not much more clothe you, O
ye of little faith?

Therefore take no thought, saying, What shall we eat? or, What shall we drink? or, Wherewithal shall we be clothed? Your heavenly Father knoweth ye have need of these things.

But seek ye first the kingdom of God and his righteousness; and all these things shall be added unto you.

Prayers
In the morning

Use me then, my Saviour, for whatever purpose and in whatever way, thou mayest require. Here is my poor heart, an empty vessel; fill it with thy grace. Here is my sinful and troubled soul; quicken it and refresh it with thy love. Take my heart for thine abode; my mouth to spread abroad the glory of thy name; my love and all my powers, for the advancement of thy believing people; and never suffer the steadfastness and confidence of my faith to abate—that so at all times I may be enabled from the heart to say, 'Jesus needs me, and I him'.

D L Moody, 1837-1899

In the evening

Be thou unto us at this time of need a tower of strength and a place of refuge. Let thy comfort support and strengthen us, thy mercy keep us, and thy grace guide us. Amen.

Primer of Henry VIII

I will lay me down in peace and take my rest, for it is thou, Lord, only that makest me to dwell in safety.

Psalm 4:5

TWELFTH DAY

We trust in the living God.

> I am trusting thee, Lord Jesus,
>   Trusting only thee;
> Trusting thee for full salvation
>   Great and free.
>
> I am trusting thee, Lord Jesus,
>   Never let me fall;
> I am trusting thee for ever
>   And for all!

Daily Reading
Psalm 40 (selected)

I waited patiently for the Lord; and he inclined unto me, and heard my cry.

He brought me up also out of a horrible pit, out of the miry clay, and set my feet upon a rock, and established my goings.

And he hath put a new song in my mouth, even praise unto our God: many shall see it, and fear, and shall trust in the Lord.

Blessed is the man that maketh the Lord his trust, and respecteth not the proud nor such as turn aside to lies.

Many, O Lord my God, are thy wonderful works which thou hast done, and thy thoughts which are to usward; they cannot be reckoned up in order unto thee: if I would declare and speak of them, they are more than can be numbered.

Let all those who seek thee rejoice and be glad in thee; let such love thy salvation say continually, The Lord be magnified.

Prayers
In the morning

O Almighty and Merciful Father, who art the help of the helpless, and the lifter up of the fallen, look down with thy mercy on all who are oppressed in mind and body; comfort and relieve them, according to their several necessities; give them patience under their sufferings, and a happy issue out of all their afflictions; and this we beg for Jesus Christ's sake. Amen.

Dean Edward Goulburn, 1818-1897

In the evening

O Lord, support us all the day long of this troublesome life, until the shadows lengthen, and the evening comes, and the busy world is hushed, the fever of life is over, and our work is done. Then, Lord, in thy mercy, grant us a safe lodging, a holy rest and peace at the last; through Jesus Christ our Lord. Amen.

Cardinal Newman, 1801-1890

THIRTEENTH DAY

As for God, his way is perfect.

> As for God, his way is perfect,
>> Know it even in thy tears,
>> Even when the mists are falling
>> On the pathway of the years,
>> And before thy clouded vision
>>> Only mystery appears.

> As for God, his way is perfect,
>> Seeing not with human sight,
>> Choosing not with human wisdom,
>> He is doing only right.
>> O remember in thy blindness
>>> God is always in the light.

Daily Reading
2 Samuel 22 (selected)

The Lord is my rock, and my fortress, and my deliverer. In my distress I called upon the Lord and he did hear my voice. He sent from above, he took me; he drew me out of many waters.

For thou art my lamp, O Lord: and the Lord will lighten my darkness.

As for God, his way is perfect; the word of the Lord is tried: he is a buckler to all them that trust in him.

For who is God, save the Lord? And who is a rock save our God?

God is my strength and power.

Thou hast enlarged my steps under me; so that my feet did not slip. Therefore I will give thanks unto thee, O Lord, I will sing praises unto thy name.

Prayers
In the morning

Almighty and Everlasting God, the comfort of the sad, the strength of them that suffer; let the prayers of thy children, who cry out of any tribulation come unto thee, and unto every soul that is distressed grant Thou mercy and relief; through Jesus Christ our Lord. Amen.

Gelasian Sacramentary, 494

In the evening

Be present, O Merciful God, and protect us through the silent hours of this night, so that we who are sick and weary may rest untroubled and unafraid; through Jesus Christ our Lord. Amen.

Ancient Collect

O God, mercifully grant unto us that the fire of thy love may burn up in us all things that displease thee, and make us meet for thy heavenly kingdom.

Roman Breviary

FOURTEENTH DAY

My God is the rock of my refuge

Rock of ages, cleft for me,
Let me hide myself in thee;
Let the water and the blood,
From thy riven side which flowed,
Be of sin the double cure;
Cleanse me from its guilt and power.

Daily Reading
Psalm 27 (selected)

The Lord is my light and my salvation; whom shall I fear?

The Lord is the strength of my life; of whom shall I be afraid?

One thing have I desired of the Lord, that will I seek after; that I may dwell in the house of the Lord all the days of my life, to behold the beauty of the Lord, and to inquire in his temple.

For in the time of trouble he shall hide me in his pavilion: in the secret of his tabernacle shall he hide me; he shall set me upon a rock.

Hear O Lord, when I cry with my voice: have mercy also upon me, and answer me.

Hide not thy face from me; and put not thy servant away in anger: thou hast been my help; leave me not, neither forsake me, O God of my salvation.

I had fainted, unless I had believed to see the goodness of the Lord in the land of the living.

Wait on the Lord: be of good courage, and he shall strengthen thine heart: wait, I say, on the Lord.

Prayers
In the morning

Almighty God, the refuge of all that are distressed, grant unto us that, in all trouble of this our mortal life, we may flee to the knowledge of thy loving-kindness and tender mercy; that so, sheltering ourselves therein, the storms of life may pass over us, and not shake the peace of God that is within us. Whatsoever this life may bring us, grant that it may never take from us the full faith that thou art our Father. Grant us thy light, that we may have life, through Jesus Christ our Lord. Amen.

George Dawson, 1821-1876

In the evening

O most merciful Redeemer, Friend and Brother,
May we know thee more clearly,
Love thee more dearly,
Follow thee more nearly,
For ever and ever. Amen.

Richard of Chichester, 1197-1253

Thine is the day, O Lord, and thine is the night. Grant that the Sun of Righteousness may abide in our hearts to drive away the darkness of evil thoughts. Amen.

Gelasian Sacramentary, 494

FIFTEENTH DAY

There is no fear in love: but perfect love casteth out fear.

> Love divine, all loves excelling,
> Joy of heaven to earth come down,
> Fix in us thy humble dwelling,
> All thy faithful mercies crown.

Daily Reading
1 Corinthians 13 (selected)

Though I speak with the tongues of men and of angels, and have not love, I am become as sounding brass or a tinkling cymbal.

And though I have the gift of prophecy, and understand all mysteries, and through all knowledge; and I have all faith, so that I could remove mountains, and have not love, I am nothing.

And though I bestow all my goods to feed the poor, and though I give my body to be burned, and have not love, it profiteth me nothing.

Love suffereth long and is kind; love envieth not; love vaunteth not itself, is not puffed up.

Doth not behave itself unseemly, seeketh not her own, is not easily provoked, thinketh no evil.

Rejoiceth not in iniquity, but rejoiceth in the truth.

Beareth all things, believeth all things, hopeth all things, endureth all things.

Love never faileth.

And now abideth faith, hope, love, these three; but the greatest of these is love.

Prayers
In the morning

O Merciful Lord, who hast made of one Blood and redeemed by one Ransome all Nations of Men, let me never harden my heart against any that partake of the same Nature and Redemption with me, but grant me an Universal Charity towards all Men.

Give me, O thou Father of Compassions, such a tenderness of Heart that I may be deeply affected with all the Miseries and Calamities outward and inward of my Brethren. Grant that I may not only seek my own things, but also the things of others. O that this mind may be in us all, which was in the Lord Jesus, that we may love as Brethren, be Pitiful and Courteous and endeavour to keep the Unity of the Spirit in the Bond of Peace, and the God of Grace, Mercy and Peace be with us all. Amen.

Thomas a Kempis, 1379-1471

In the evening

Almighty and Everlasting God, who dost en-
kindle the flame of thy love in the hearts of the
Saints, grant us to our minds the same faith and
power of love; that as we rejoice in their
triumphs, we may profit by their examples;
through Jesus Christ our Lord. Amen.

Gothic Missal

SIXTEENTH DAY

Rest in the Lord, and wait patiently for him.

Rest of the weary, Joy of the sad;
Hope of the dreary, Light of the glad;
Home of the stranger, Strength to the end;
Refuge from danger, Saviour and Friend.

Daily Reading
Psalm 37 (selected)

Fret not thyself because of evil-doers, neither be
thou envious against the workers of iniquity.

Trust in the Lord, and do good: so shalt thou
dwell in the land, and verily thou shalt be fed.

Delight thyself also in the Lord: and he shall
give thee the desires of thine heart.

Commit thy way unto the Lord; trust also in
him; and he shall bring it to pass.

Rest in the Lord, and wait patiently for him.

The steps of a good man are ordered by the Lord: and he delighteth in his way.

Though he fall, he shall not be utterly cast down: for the Lord upholdeth him with his hand.

I have been young, and now am old; yet have I not seen the righteous forsaken, nor his seed begging bread.

But the salvation of the righteous is of the Lord: he is their strength in the time of trouble, and the Lord shall help them and deliver them: and save them, because they trust in him.

Prayers
In the morning

Lord Jesus, grant us daily grace for daily need; daily patience for a daily cross; daily, hourly incessant love to thee to take up our cross daily and bear it after thee. We ask this for thine own Name's sake.

Christina G Rossetti, 1830-1894

Comfort, O merciful Father, by thy Word and Holy Spirit, all who are afflicted or distressed, and so turn their hearts unto thee, that they may serve thee in truth and bring forth fruit to thy glory. Be thou, O Lord, their succour and defence; through Jesus Christ our Lord. Amen.

Philip Melanchton, 1497-1560

In the evening

Grant us thy peace, Lord, through the coming
    night,
Turn thou for us its darkness into light;
From harm and danger keep thy children free,
For dark and light are both alike to thee.

John Ellerton, 1826-1893

Be present, O merciful God, and protect us
through the silent hours of this night, so that we
who are wearied by the changes of this fleeting
world may rest upon thy eternal changelessness;
through Jesus Christ our Lord. Amen.

Gelasian Sacramentary, 494

SEVENTEENTH DAY

The Lord shall guide thee continually.

> I am trusting thee to guide me;
> Thou alone shalt lead,
> Every day and hour supplying
> All my need.

Daily Reading
John 14 (selected)

Jesus said, I am the Way, the Truth and the Life;
no man cometh unto the Father but by me.

If ye love me, keep my commandments, and I will pray to the Father, and he shall give you another comforter, that he may abide with you for ever; even the Spirit of Truth, whom the world cannot receive, because it seeth him not, neither knoweth him; but ye know him; for he dwelleth with you, and shall be in you.

I will not leave you comfortless: I will come to you.

He that hath my commandments, and keepeth them, he it is that loveth me: and he that loveth me shall be loved of my Father, and I will love him and will manifest myself to him.

If a man love me, he will keep my words: and my Father will love him, and we will come unto him, and make our abode with him.

Peace I leave with you, my peace I give unto you; not as the world giveth, give I unto you. Let not your heart be troubled, neither let it be afraid.

Prayers
In the morning

O most loving Father, who willest us to give thanks for all things, to dread nothing but loss of thee, and to cast all our care on thee, who carest for us, preserve us from fears and anxieties, and grant that no clouds of this mortal life may hide us from the light of that Love which is immortal, and which thou hast manifested unto us in thy Son, Jesus Christ our Lord. Amen.

William Bright, 1824-1901

In the evening

Abide with me from morn till eve,
For without thee I cannot live:
Abide with me when night is nigh,
For without thee I dare not die.

John Keble, 1792-1866

Almighty and Everlasting God, the Comfort of
the sad, the Strength of sufferers, let the prayers
of those that cry out of any tribulation come
unto thee, that all may rejoice to find that thy
mercy is present with them in their afflictions:
through Jesus Christ our Lord. Amen.

Gelasian Sacramentary, 494

EIGHTEENTH DAY

*He that dwelleth in the secret place of the Most High
shall abide under the shadow of the Almighty.*

My heart is resting, O my God;
I will give thanks and sing;
My heart is at the secret source,
Of every precious thing.

Daily Reading
John 15 (selected)

I am the true vine, and my Father is the hus-
band-man. Every branch in me that beareth not
fruit he taketh away; and every branch that

35

beareth fruit, he purgeth it, that it may bring forth more fruit.

Abide in me, and I in you. As the branch cannot bear fruit of itself, except it abide in the vine: no more can ye, except ye abide in me.

I am the vine, ye are the branches; he that abideth in me, and I in him, the same bringeth forth much fruit: for without me ye can do nothing.

If ye abide in me, and my words abide in you, ye shall ask what ye will, and it shall be done unto you.

As my Father hath loved me, so have I loved you: continue ye in my love.

If ye keep my commandments, ye shall abide in my love: even as I have kept my Father's commandments and abide in his love. This is my commandment, That ye love one another, as I have loved you.

Prayers
In the morning

Grant me I beseech thee, O merciful God, ardently to desire, prudently to study, rightly to understand, and perfectly to fulfil, that which is pleasing to thee, to the praise and Glory of thy name.

Thomas Aquinas, 1226-1274

O Lord Heavenly Father, in whom is the fulness of light and wisdom: enlighten our minds by thy Holy Spirit, and give us grace to receive thy

Word with reverence and humility, without which no man can understand thy truth; for Christ's sake. Amen.

John Calvin, 1509-1564

In the evening

O thou, who art the Light of the minds that know thee, the Life of the souls that love thee, and the Strength of the thoughts that seek thee: help us to know thee, that we may truly love thee, so to love thee, that we may fully serve thee, whose service is perfect freedom: through Jesus Christ our Lord. Amen.

Gelasian Sacramentary, 494

NINETEENTH DAY

All thy waves and thy billows are gone over me.

> Jesus Saviour, pilot me,
> Over life's tempestuous sea;
> Unknown waves before me roll
> Hiding rock and treacherous shoal;
> Chart and compass come from thee,
> Jesus Saviour, pilot me.

Daily Reading
Psalm 69 (selected)

Save me, O God; for the waters are come in unto my soul.

I sink in deep mire, where there is no standing: I am come unto deep waters, where the floods overflow me.

I am weary of my crying: my throat is dried: mine eyes fail while I wait for my God.

O God thou knowest my foolishness: and my sins are not hid from thee.

Deliver me out of the mire, and let me not sink: let me be delivered out of the deep waters.

Let not the waterflood overflow me, neither let the deep swallow me up, and let not the pit shut her mouth upon me.

Hear me, O Lord; for thy loving-kindness is good: turn unto me according to the multitude of thy tender mercies: and hide not thy face from thy servant; for I am in trouble: hear me speedily.

Prayers
In the morning

We thank thee, O God, for those who have travlled over the tempestuous seas of this life and have made the harbour of peace and felicity.

Watch over us, who are still on our dangerous voyage: and remember such as lie exposed to the rough storms of trouble and temptation.

Frail is our vessel and the ocean is wide: but

in thy mercy thou hast set our course, so steer the vessel of our life toward the everlasting shore of peace, and bring us at length to the quiet haven of our heart's desire, where thou, O our God, art blessed and livest and reignest for ever and ever. Amen.

St Augustine, 354-430

In the evening

Thou hast made us for thyself, O Lord, and our hearts are restless until they find rest in thee. Grant us we pray.

> In all our duties, thy help:
> In all our perplexities, thy guidance:
> In all our dangers, thy protection:
> In all our sorrows, thy peace:
> Through Jesus Christ our Lord.

St Augustine, 354-430

TWENTIETH DAY

Come unto Me, all ye that labour and are heavy laden, and I will give you rest.

> There's a wideness in God's mercy.
> Like the wideness of the sea:
> There's a kindness in his justice,
> Which is more than liberty.

For the love of God is broader
Than the measure of man's mind,
And the heart of the Eternal,
Is most wonderfully kind.

Daily Reading
Luke 15:1-7

Then drew near unto him all the publicans and sinners for to hear him. And the Pharisees and scribes murmured saying, This man receiveth sinners, and eateth with them.

And he spoke this parable unto them, saying, What man of you having an hundred sheep, if he lose one of them, doth not leave the ninety and nine in the wilderness, and go after that which is lost, until he find it?

And when he hath found it, he layeth it on his shoulders, rejoicing. And when he cometh home, he calleth together his friends and neighbours, saying unto them, Rejoice with me: for I have found my sheep which was lost.

I say unto you, that likewise, joy shall be in heaven over one sinner that repenteth, more than over ninety and nine just persons, which need no repentance.

Prayers
In the morning

Into thy hands, O Lord, we commend our spirits, souls and bodies, for thou has created and redeemed them. O Lord God Almighty, guide us and all whom we love, and kindle thy light in our hearts, that thy goodly knowledge increasing in us more and more, we may always be found to walk and live after thy will and pleasure; through Jesus Christ our Lord. Amen.

Ancient Collect

In the evening

Blessed Lord, who for our sakes wast content to bear sorrow and want and death; grant unto us such a measure of thy Spirit that we may follow thee in all self-denial and tenderness of soul. Help us by thy great Love, to succour the afflicted, to relieve the needy and destitute, to share the burdens of heavy laden, and ever to see thee in all that are poor and desolate. Amen.

Bishop Westcott, 1825-1901

TWENTY-FIRST DAY

Are not two sparrows sold for a farthing? And one of them shall not fall to the ground without your Father's will. Fear ye not therefore, ye are of more value than many sparrows.

Thine for ever! Lord of life,
Shield us through our early strife,
Thou the Life, the Truth, the Way,
Guard us to the realms of day.

Daily Reading
Psalm 139 (selected)

O Lord thou hast searched me, and known me,
Thou knowest my downsitting and mine uprising,
Thou understandest my thought afar off
Thou compassest my path and my lying down,
And art aquainted with all my ways.
For there is not a word in my tongue,
But, lo, O Lord, thou knowest it altogether
Thou hast beset me behind and before,
And laid thy hand upon me,
Such knowledge is too wonderful for me;
It is high, I cannot attain unto it,
Whither shall I go from thy Spirit?
Or whither shall I flee from thy presence?
If I ascend up into heaven, thou art there:
If I make my bed in hell, behold, thou art there.
If I take the wings of the morning,
And dwell in the uttermost parts of the sea;
Even there shall thy hand lead me,
And thy right hand shall hold me.

Prayers
In the morning

Our God and loving Father, thy presence is ever
with us; wheresoever we seek we find thee, in
our homes, in the fields, in the temple, and in
the highway. Whatsoever we do, thou art with
us, whether we eat or drink, whether we write
or work, read, meditate or pray, thou art with
us. Wheresoever we are or whatsoever we do,
we feel some measure of thy mercies and thy

love. If we be oppressed, thou defendest us; if we hunger, thou feedest us. Whatsoever we need, thou givest us. O continue this loving-kindness toward us, through Jesus Christ our Lord. Amen.

J Norden, 1548-1600

In the evening

O thou, who so carest for every one of us, as if thou carest for him alone; and so for all, as if all were but one! I behold how some things pass away that others may replace them, but thou dost never depart. Thou hast made us for thyself, O Lord, and our hearts are restless until they find rest in thee.

St Augustine, 354-430

TWENTY-SECOND DAY

God shall supply all your need.

> The Saviour calls: let every ear
> Attend the heavenly sound:
> Ye doubting souls, dismiss your fear,
> Hope smiles reviving round.
>
> For every thirsty, longing heart,
> Here streams of bounty flow:
> And life and health, and bliss impart,
> To banish mortal woe.

43

Daily Reading
Isaiah 55 (selected)

Ho, every one that thirsteth, come ye to the waters, and he that hath no money; come ye, buy and eat; yea, come, buy wine and milk without money and without price.

Wherefore do you spend money for that which is not bread? and your labour for that which satisfieth not? Hearken diligently unto me, and eat ye that which is good, and let your souls delight itself in fatness.

Seek ye the Lord while he may be found, call ye upon him while he is near.

Let the wicked forsake his way, and the unrighteous man his thoughts: and let him return unto the Lord, and he will have mercy upon him: and to our God for he will abundantly pardon.

For ye shall go out with joy, and be led forth with peace: the mountains and the hills shall break forth before you into singing, and all the trees of the field shall clap their hands.

Prayers
In the morning

O Lord, our God, great, eternal, wonderful in glory, who keepest covenant and promise for those that love thee with their whole heart, who art the life of all, the help of those that flee unto thee, the hope of those who cry unto thee.

Cleanse us from our sins, and from every

thought displeasing to thy goodness, cleanse our souls and bodies, our hearts and consciences, that with a pure heart and a clean mind, with perfect love and calm hope, we may venture confidently and fearlessly to pray unto thee; through Jesus Christ our Lord. Amen.

Liturgy of St Basil, c. 330-379

In the evening

Guide me, teach me, strengthen me, till I become such a person as thou wouldst have me be; pure and gentle, truthful and high minded, brave and able, courteous and generous, dutiful and useful. Amen.

Charles Kingsley, 1819-1875

TWENTY-THIRD DAY

Cause me to know the way wherein I should walk, for I lift up my soul unto thee. In thee do I trust.

I lift my heart to thee,
Saviour divine;
For all thou art to me,
And I am thine.
Is there on earth a closer bond than this,
That, 'my beloved's mine, and I am his?'

Daily Reading
Psalm 25 (selected)

Unto thee, O Lord, do I lift up my soul. O my God I trust in thee. Show me thy ways, O Lord; teach me thy paths. Lead me in thy truth, and teach me: for thou art the God of my salvation; on thee do I wait all the day.

Remember, O Lord, thy tender mercies and thy loving-kindness: for they have been ever of old.

Remember not the sins of my youth, nor my transgressions: according to thy mercy remember thou me for thy goodness sake, O Lord. For thy name's sake, O Lord, pardon mine iniquity; for it is great.

What man is he that feareth the Lord? Him shall he teach in the way that he shall choose.

The secret of the Lord is with them that fear him, and he will show them his covenant.

Look upon mine affliction and my pain; and forgive all my sins. O keep my soul, and deliver me; for I put my trust in thee.

Prayers
In the morning

Merciful Father, to all thy dispensations we would submit ourselves and not merely of necessity, but because we believe in thy wisdom and thy goodness. In bereavement and in sorrow, in death as in life, in joys and in happiness, we would see thy hand. Teach us to see it; increase our faith where we cannot see; teach us also to love justice, and to do mercy, and to walk humbly with thee our God. Make us at peace with all mankind, gentle to those who offend us, faithful in all duties. Make us loving to one another, patient in distress, and ever thankful to thy Divine power, which keeps and guides, and blesses us every day. Let thy peace reign in our hearts and enable us to walk with thee in love; through Jesus Christ our Lord. Amen.

Francis H Newman, 1805-1897

In the evening

Sun of my soul, thou Saviour dear,
It is not night if thou be near;
Oh, may no earth-born cloud arise,
To hide thee from thy servant's eyes.

Come near and bless us when we wake,
Ere through the world our way we take;
Till in the ocean of thy love,
We lose ourselves in heaven above.

John Keble, 1792-1866

TWENTY-FOURTH DAY

Fear not: for behold I bring you good tidings of great joy, which shall be to all people.

He comes the broken heart to bind,
The bleeding soul to cure,
And with the treasures of his grace
To enrich the humble poor.

Daily Reading
Luke 4:16-21

And he came to Nazareth, where he had been brought up, and he entered, as his custom was, into the synagogue on the Sabbath day, and stood up to read. And there was delivered unto him the book of the prophet Isaiah. And he opened the book and found the place where it was written:

The Spirit of the Lord is upon me.
Because he hath anointed me to preach good tidings to the poor:
He hath sent me to proclaim release to the captives,
And recovering of sight to the blind
To set at liberty them that are bruised,
To proclaim the acceptable year of the Lord.

And he closed the book and gave it back to the attendant, and sat down: and the eyes of all in the synagogue were fastened on him. And he began to say unto them, Today hath this scripture been fulfilled in your ears.

Prayers
In the morning

O Lord, come quickly and reign on thy throne, for now oft-times something rises up within me, and tries to take possession of thy throne; pride, covetousness, uncleanness, and sloth want to be my kings; and then evil-speaking, anger, hatred, and the whole train of vices join with me in warring against myself, and try to reign over me. I resist them. I cry out against them, and say 'I have no other King than Christ'. O King of peace, come and reign in me, for I will have no king but thee! Amen.

St Bernard, 1091-1153

In the evening

O God, the Father of lights, from whom cometh down every good and perfect gift, have mercy on our frailty, and grant us such health of body as thou knowest to be needful for us; that both in our bodies and our souls we may evermore serve thee with all our strength and might; through Jesus Christ our Lord. Amen.

Bishop Cosin, 1594-1672

TWENTY-FIFTH DAY

All thy works shall praise thee, O Lord; and thy saints shall bless thee.

> When all thy mercies, O my God,
> My rising soul surveys,
> Transported with the view, I'm lost
> In wonder, love and praise.

Daily Reading
Psalm 19:7-14

The law of the Lord is perfect, converting the
  soul:
The testimony of the Lord is sure, making
  wise the simple,
The statutes of the Lord are right, rejoicing
  the heart:
The commandment of the Lord is pure,
  enlightening the eyes.
The fear of the Lord is clean, enduring for
  ever:
The judgments of the Lord are true and
  righteous altogether
More to be desired are they than gold, yea,
  than much fine gold:
Sweeter also than honey and the honeycomb,
Moreover by them is thy servant warned:
And in keeping of them there is great reward.
Who can understand his errors?
Cleanse thou me from secret faults,
Keep back thy servant also from presumpt-
  uous sins;
Let them not have dominion over me:
Then shall I be upright,
And I shall be innocent from the great trans-
  gression.
Let the words of my mouth, and the
  meditation of my heart, be acceptable in
  thy sight,
O Lord my strength, and my redeemer.

Prayers
In the morning

O Lord God, thou art my Glory and the exult-
ation of my heart; thou art my Hope and Refuge
in the day of my trouble. Set me free from all
evil passions, that being inwardly cured and
thoroughly cleansed, I may be made fit to love,
courageous to suffer, steady to persevere.
Nothing is sweeter than love, nothing more
courageous, nothing fuller nor better in heaven
and earth; because love is born of God, and
cannot rest but in God, above all created things.
Let me love thee more than myself, nor love
myelf, but for thee. Amen.

Thomas a Kempis, 1379-1471

In the evening

Give us, O Lord, a steadfast heart, which no unworthy affection may drag downwards; give us
an unconquered heart, which no tribulation can
wear out; give us an upright heart, which no
unworthy purpose may tempt aside.

Bestow upon us also, O Lord our God,
understanding to know thee, diligence to seek
thee, wisdom to find thee, and a faithfulness
that may finally embrace thee; through Jesus
Christ our Lord. Amen.

Thomas Aquinas, 1226-1274

TWENTY-SIXTH DAY

Be ye all of one mind, having compassion one of another; and be not weary in well-doing.

> Go labour on, spend and be spent,
> Thy joy to do the Father's will;
> It is the way the Master went,
> Should not the servant tread it still?

Daily Reading
Matthew 25 (selected)

Then shall the King say to those on his right hand, Come you blessed of my Father, inherit the kingdom prepared for you from the foundation of the world:

For I was hungry and you fed me: I was thirsty and you gave me to drink: I was a stranger and you entertained me: I was naked and you clothed me: I was ill and you looked after me: I was in prison and you visited me.

Then they will answer him saying, Lord when did we see you hungry and feed you? or thirsty and gave you to drink? When did we see you a stranger and entertain you? or naked and clothe you? Or when did we see you sick or in prison and visit you?

And the King will answer and say to them, I tell you truly in so far as you did it to one of the least of these my brothers, you did it unto me.

Prayers
In the morning

O Lord, who though thou wast rich, yet for our sakes didst become poor, and has promised in thy gospel that whatsoever is done unto the least of thy brethren, thou wilt receive as done unto thee; give us grace, we humbly beseech thee, to be ever willing and ready to minister, as thou enablest us, to the necessities of our fellow-creatures, and to extend the blessings of thy kingdom over all the world, to thy praise and glory, who art God over all, blessed for ever. Amen.

St Augustine, 354-430

In the evening

O Lord, renew our spirits and draw our hearts unto thyself that our work may not be to us as a burden, but a delight; and give us such a mighty love to thee as may sweeten all our obedience. O let us not serve thee with the spirit of bondage as slaves, but in the cheerfulness and gladness of children, delighting ourselves in thee and rejoicing in thy work. Amen.

Benjamin Jenks, 1646-1724

TWENTY-SEVENTH DAY

Let all the world in every corner sing, 'My God and King'.

> Praise my soul, the King of heaven;
> To his feet thy tribute bring;
> Ransomed, healed, restored, forgiven,
> Who like me his praise should sing?

Daily Reading
Psalm 103 (selected)

Bless the Lord, O my soul: and all that is within me, bless his holy name.

Bless the Lord, O my soul, and forget not all his benefits:

Who forgiveth all thine iniquities; who healeth all thy diseases;

Who redeemeth thy life from destruction; who crowneth thee with loving-kindness and tender mercies;

Who satisfieth thy mouth with good things; so that thy youth is renewed like the eagle's.

The Lord is merciful and gracious, slow to anger, and plenteous in mercy.

He hath not dealt with us after our sins; nor rewarded us according to our iniquities.

For as the heaven is high above the earth, so great is his mercy toward them that fear him.

As far as the east is from the west, so far hath he removed our transgressions from us.

Like as a father pitieth his children, so the Lord pitieth them that fear him.

The mercy of the Lord is from everlasting to everlasting upon them that fear him, and to those who remember his commandments to do them.

Prayers
In the morning

Almighty God, of thy fulness, grant unto us who need so much, thy wisdom and strength. Bring our wills unto thine. Lift our understandings into thy heavenly light; that we thereby beholding those things which are right, and being drawn by thy love, may bring our will and our understanding together to thy service, until at last, body and soul and spirit may be all thine, and thou be our Father and our Eternal Friend. Amen.

George Dawson, 1821-1876

In the evening

O Lord God, Father of Light, if I say, Surely the darkness will cover me; even the night shall be light about me. Yea, the darkness hideth not from thee; but the night shineth as the day; the darkness and the light are both alike unto thee. Therefore, I will lay me down in peace and sleep: for thou, Lord, only makest me to dwell in safety. Amen.

Psalm 3 and 139

TWENTY-EIGHTH DAY

For God so loved the world, that he gave his only begotten Son, that whosoever believeth in him should not perish but have everlasting life.

And so the Word had flesh, and wrought
With human hands the creed of creeds,
In loveliness of perfect deeds,
More strong than all poetic thoughts.

Daily Readings
John I:1-12

In the beginning was the Word, and the Word was with God, and the Word was God.

The same was in the beginning with God. All things were made by him; and without him was not anything made that was made.

In him was life; and the life was the light of men. And the light shineth in darkness; and the darkness has never quenched it.

There was a man sent from God, whose name was John. The same came for a witness, to bear witness of the Light, that all men through him might believe.

He was not that Light, but was sent to bear witness of that Light. That was the true Light, which lighteth every man that cometh into the world.

He was in the world, and the world was made by him, and the world know him not.

He came unto his own, and his own received him not. But as many as received him, to them gave he power to become the sons of God, even to them that believe on his Name.

Prayers
In the morning

To thee, O God, we call out and speak. Hear us, O Lord, for thou art our Lord and our God. Enlighten our minds to understand the meaning of thy Word. Forgive us our lack of comprehension of all that thy Gospel means; but at least this we do know, that we love thee—Yea, love thee above all other things. We seek thee, we follow thee, we are ready to serve thee: under thy power we desire to abide, for thou art the Saviour and Sovereign of all. We pray thee to command us as thou wilt; through Jesus Christ our Lord. Amen.

King Alfred, 849-901

In the evening

Teach us Good Lord—
To serve thee as thou deservest;
To give and not to count the cost;
To fight and not to heed the wounds;
To toil and not to seek for rest;
To labour and not to ask for any reward,
Save that of knowing that we do thy will.
Amen.

Ignatius Loyola, 1491-1556

TWENTY-NINTH DAY

Let my mouth be filled with thy praise.

> Lord speak to me, that I may speak
> In living echoes, of thy tone;
> As thou hast sought, so let me seek
> Thy erring children, lost and lone.
>
> O strengthen me, that, while I stand
> Firm on the rock, and strong in thee,
> I may stretch out a loving hand
> To wrestlers with the troubled sea.

Daily Reading
Ephesians (selected)

Blessed be the God and Father of our Lord Jesus Christ, who hath blessed us with all spiritual blessings: and you hath he quickened, who were dead in trespasses and sins. For by grace are ye saved through faith; and that not of yourselves: it is the gift of God.

I pray the Father of our Lord Jesus Christ, that he would grant you, according to the riches of his glory, to be stengthened with might by his Spirit in the inner man; that Christ may dwell in your hearts by faith; that ye being rooted and grounded in love, may be able to comprehend with all the saints what is the breadth and length, and depth and height; and to know the love of Christ, which passeth knowledge, that ye might be filled with all the fulness of God.

Now unto him who is able to do exceeding abundantly above all that we can ask or think, according to the power that worketh in us, unto him be the glory in the church by Jesus Christ throughout all ages, world without end.

Prayers
In the morning

O thou plenteous Source of every good and perfect gift, shed abroad the cheering light of thy sevenfold grace over our hearts. Yea, Spirit of love and gentleness, we most humbly implore thy assistance. Thou knowest our faults, our failings, our necessities, the dullness of our understanding, the waywardness of our affections, the perverseness of our will. When, therefore, we neglect to practise what we know, visit us, we beseech thee, with thy grace, enlighten our minds, rectify our desires, correct our wanderings, and pardon our omissions, so that by thy guidance we may be preserved from making shipwreck of faith, and may at length be landed safe in the haven of eternal rest; through Jesus Christ our Lord. Amen.

Anselm, 1033-1109

In the evening

Lord God Almighty, I pray thee of thy great mercy to guide me to thy will, that above all things I may inwardly love thee with a clean mind and a clean body; for thou art my Maker, my Help and my Hope. Amen.

King Alfred, 849-901

O thou who hast given us so much, mercifully grant us one thing more—a grateful heart; for Christ's sake. Amen.

George Herbert, 1593-1633

THIRTIETH DAY

Him that cometh unto Me, I will in no wise cast out.

> Art thou weary, art thou languid,
> Art thou sore distressed?
> 'Come to Me,' saith One, 'and coming,
> Be at rest.'
>
> If I ask him to receive me,
> Will he say me nay?
> Not till earth and not till heaven
> Pass away.

Daily Reading
Luke 19:1-10

And Jesus entered and passed through Jericho. And behold, there was a man named Zaccheus, who was chief among the tax-gatherers and very rich. He was eager to see what Jesus looked like: but being a little man, he could not see him for the crowd. So he ran on ahead and climbed into a sycamore tree in order to see him for Jesus was to pass that way.

When Jesus came to the place, he looked up and said, 'Zaccheus, be quick and come down: I must come and stay with you today'. Zaccheus climbed down as fast as he could and welcomed him gladly. At this there was a general murmur of disapproval. 'He has gone in,' they said, 'to be the guest of a sinner.' But Zaccheus stood there and said to the Lord, 'Behold, sir, here and now I give half of my goods to the poor; and if I have cheated anyone, I am ready to pay him fourfold'. And Jesus said to him, 'This day is salvation come to this house, for this man too is a son of Abraham.

For 'the Son of Man is come to seek and to save that which was lost'.

Prayers
In the morning

O Lord, in whose hands are life and death, by whose power I am sustained, and by whose mercy I am spared, look down upon me with pity. Forgive me that I have until now so much neglected the duty which thou hast assigned to me, and suffered the days and hours of which I must give account to pass away without any endeavour to accomplish thy will. Make me to remember, O God, that every day is thy gift, and ought to be used according to thy command.

Grant me, therefore, so to repent of my negligence, that I may obtain mercy from thee, and pass the time which thou shalt yet allow me in diligent performance of thy commands; through Jesus Christ our Lord. Amen.

Samuel Johnson, 1709-1784

In the evening

O Lord our God, grant us grace to desire thee with our whole heart; that so desiring we may seek and find thee; and so finding thee may love thee; and loving thee, may hate those sins from which thou has redeemed us. Amen.

Anselm, 1033-1109

THIRTY-FIRST DAY

The same yesterday, and today, and for ever.

O God our help in ages past,
Our hope for years to come,
Our shelter from the stormy blast,
And our eternal home.

Before the hills in order stood,
Or earth received its frame,
From everlasting thou art God,
To endless years the same.

Daily Reading
Psalm 90 (selected)

Lord, thou hast been our dwelling place in all generations. Before the mountains were brought forth, or ever thou hadst formed the earth and the world, even from everlasting to everlasting, thou art God.

For a thousand years in thy sight are but as yesterday when it is past, and as a watch in the night.

Thou carriest them away as with a flood; they are as a sleep: in the morning they are like grass which groweth up. In the morning it flourisheth and groweth up; in the evening it is cut down and withereth.

We spend our years as a tale that is told.

So teach us to number our days, that we may apply our hearts unto wisdom.

O satisfy us early with thy mercy; that we may rejoice and be glad all our days. And let the beauty of the Lord our God be upon us: and establish thou the work of our hands upon us: yea, the work of our hands establish thou it.

Prayers
In the morning

O Lord, thou knowest what is best for us, let this or that be done as thou shalt please. Give what thou wilt, and how much thou wilt, and when thou wilt.

Deal with me as thou thinkest good, and as best pleaseth thee. Behold, I am thy servant, prepared for all things: for I desire not to live unto myself, but unto thee; and O that I could do it more worthily and perfectly! Amen.

Thomas a Kempis, 1379-1471

In the evening

O gracious and holy Father, give us—
Wisdom to perceive thee;
Intelligence to understand thee;
Diligence to seek thee;
Patience to wait for thee;
Eyes to behold thee;
A heart to meditate upon thee;
And a life to proclaim thee;

Through the power of the Spirit of Jesus Christ our Lord. Amen.

St Benedict, 480-543